Teacher's Notes for Guided Reading

The Burglar's Breakfast

Teacher's notes by Alison Kelly
Roehampton University
and Suzanne Maile
Sheen Mount School

Contents

Essential information

National Curriculum level: 2B

Genre: Story with familiar setting / humorous

Word count: 1013

High frequency words

a/an	about	and	as	at	back	be
been	big	but	by	came	can	could
day	did	do	door	down	first	from
get	good	had	has	have	he	him
his	home	house	I	in	it	just
last	make	more	night	no	now	of
off	on	one	out	put	ran	than
that	the	their	them	then	there	they
three	time	to	two	up	very	want
was	way	went	were	what	when	where
who	with	would				

Interest words and phrases

strode	snaffled	scrambled	'cool head'	detective

Background

Inept burglar Alfie Briggs has the tables turned on him when he finds his breakfast has been stolen. This cleverly patterned book narrates his efforts to detect each missing item, and the change of heart which leads to a new career – as a detective!

Introducing the story

Before you start the reading session or sessions, spend a little time preparing with your group.

You might like to bring in some props: "burglar" props, such as a mask, striped jersey, torch and swag bag; "detective" props such as a magnifying glass and (if you can find one, possibly in a costume department or novelty shop) Sherlock Holmes-style deerstalker hat.

Or use "breakfast" as your starting point: bring in props or pictures, and discuss the children's favourite breakfast foods.

Share learning objectives with your group.

The children are going to learn or practise the following:

- to use deductive skills
- to use syntax and context to support decoding of new words.

You might say:

- We are going to practise working things out from clues, just like detectives.
- We are going to practise learning to read new words from what we have already read or what we already know.

Show the children a copy of the book.

Identify the text type: (humorous) fiction.

Look at the front cover. Ask questions such as:

- What is the title of the book?
- Do you know any other stories about burglars?

Ask children for their initial predictions. For instance:

- What do you think might happen in this story?

Read the back cover blurb.

- What do you think now about the story?

Give a brief introduction to the book. For example:

We are going to read a story about a burglar who loves his breakfasts – but one morning doesn't go exactly as he planned...

Now go on to the Walkthrough (see overleaf).

Walkthrough

The walkthrough allows you to "warm" the text for the children by taking them through it without actually reading it.

- You might use it to identify key vocabulary, language patterns and concepts that children could need support with
- You can identify phoneme-grapheme relationships that are to be practised
- It can be a way to identify key 'thinking points' in the story (e.g. where predictions might be made, characters' thoughts inferred and so on).

Using a copy of the book, look through it with the children. We have suggested pause points and prompts.

Chapter 1

Breakfast!

Alfie Briggs was a burglar.
But he wasn't a good one.
Tonight, he'd stolen a broken
lawn mower and a bird...

3

Page 3

You might say:

- Here's Alfie Briggs. The book says he wasn't a good burglar. Can you tell that from the picture?

Go on to pages 6-7.

You might say:

- Alfie's best meal of the day is breakfast. Why do you think that is?
- Let's find Alfie's favourite foods.
  (They are to be found on labels around the room – children can spot these and read with you.)
- What clues do we get about Alfie from looking round his kitchen? Is he a tidy and organized person, do you think?

Move on to chapters 2 - 3. Walk through these chapters which set the pattern for the rest of the book:

- Oh dear, he's lost his cornflakes (find the word "cornflakes"). Now he's following the trail; now he seems to have found what happened to them...

Chapter 2

No breakfast...

Alfie's stomach gave a hungry growl. It was time for breakfast.

Mmm. What shall I have first? Cornflakes I think.

He hunted high...

8

...and low. But he couldn't find the cornflakes.

That's funny. I thought I had a box left.

9

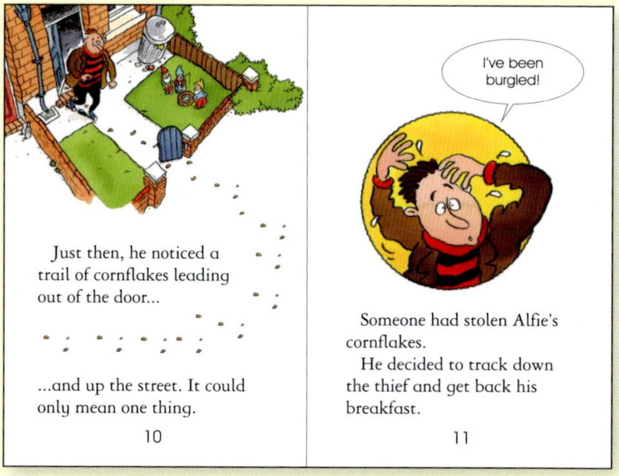

Just then, he noticed a trail of cornflakes leading out of the door...

...and up the street. It could only mean one thing.

10

I've been burgled!

Someone had stolen Alfie's cornflakes.

He decided to track down the thief and get back his breakfast.

11

Chapter 3

On the trail

Nose pressed against his magnifying glass, Alfie followed the cornflake trail.

He followed the trail into the park. He followed it to Pets' Corner. The thief would be sorry he'd stolen from Alfie.

13

Suddenly, Alfie came face to face with the thief. The thief looked even grumpier than Alfie. What's more, he had two sharp horns.

14

"Er, nice goat!" said Alfie. The goat glared. Perhaps he didn't like having his breakfast interrupted.

The fox ran off. Alfie spotted something.

Alfie was cross. First, his cornflakes had been snaffled by a greedy goat. Now his plan for eggs had been scrambled by a cheeky fox.

He stomped home. He flung open his front door. Then he stormed into the kitchen.

21

Page 21

Check that the children understand the vocabulary – snaffled, scrambled, stomped.

NEED A JOB?

Can you:
Follow trails?
Track down stolen goods?
Catch crooks?
Spot clues?
Keep a cool head?

The STOP-A-THIEF
Detective Agency
needs
YOU!

38

"Can I follow trails?" thought Alfie, remembering his trip to the park.

39

Move on to page 38.

Check the children's understanding of the phrase "cool head".

Independent reading and strategy check

Before the children begin reading, include a strategy check to help them tackle difficult or unfamiliar words. **You might say:**

- Let's remember what we do when we can't read a word.
  Elicit suggestions from the children, e.g. blend the phonemes, read ahead.

Ask the children to read aloud, a little at a time, either all together or in turns, whilst you listen and monitor. Encourage them to use cues to work out unfamiliar words, and praise fluent reading or good use of strategies.

For assessment purposes, you may want to use the chart on pages 30-31 to note strategies that each child uses, or errors or comments that he or she makes, during the reading.

Now ask the children to read Chapters 1-4 (i.e. up to page 27) whilst you monitor and record strategies.

Chapter 1

Breakfast!

Alfie Briggs was a burglar. But he wasn't a good one. Tonight, he'd stolen a broken lawn mower and a bird...

3

...a talking bird. It almost woke up the whole street.

After a hard night, Alfie liked to go home to a tasty breakfast.

Breakfast was his main meal of the day. He always ate at least three courses.

5

He tried to make sure he never ran out of the five breakfast foods he liked best.

Looking around his kitchen, it was easy to see what they were.

7

Chapter 2

No breakfast...

Alfie's stomach gave a hungry growl. It was time for breakfast.

He hunted high...

8

...and low. But he couldn't find the cornflakes.

9

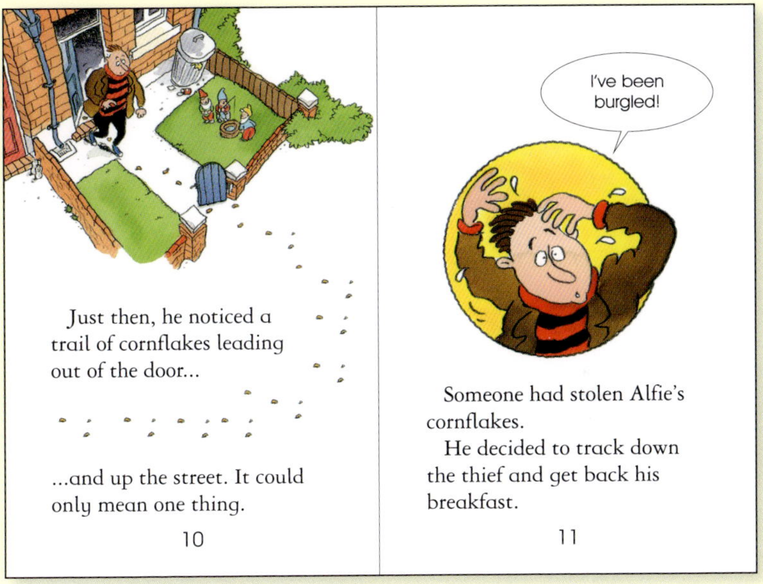

Just then, he noticed a trail of cornflakes leading out of the door...

...and up the street. It could only mean one thing.

10

Someone had stolen Alfie's cornflakes.

He decided to track down the thief and get back his breakfast.

11

Chapter 3

On the trail

Nose pressed against his magnifying glass, Alfie followed the cornflake trail.

Pause after page 12.

You could ask:

- What's Alfie doing now? Is he still being a burglar?
- Look at the signpost in the picture. Which way do you think Alfie will go?

Now ask the children to read pages 13 - 21.

He followed the trail into the park. He followed it to Pets' Corner. The thief would be sorry he'd stolen from Alfie.

13

Suddenly, Alfie came face to face with the thief. The thief looked even grumpier than Alfie. What's more, he had two sharp horns.

14

"Er, nice goat!" said Alfie. The goat glared. Perhaps he didn't like having his breakfast interrupted.

On his way home, Alfie thought about what he'd have for breakfast instead of cornflakes.

Feeling happier, he strode along when crunch! Alfie stepped on a broken egg shell beside the hedge.

"Someone else has had the same idea!" he said and grinned.

He thought he knew who that someone was.

17

Alfie knelt down. He crawled through a hole in the hedge. On the other side were more broken shells and one happy fox.

The fox ran off. Alfie spotted something.

Alfie was cross. First, his cornflakes had been snaffled by a greedy goat. Now his plan for eggs had been scrambled by a cheeky fox.

He stomped home. He flung open his front door. Then he stormed into the kitchen.

21

Pause after page 21.

You could say:

- Alfie has come home in a very bad mood. What do you think he'll find in his kitchen?

Now ask the children to read pages 22-27.

Chapter 4

Cat and mouse

"Right," Alfie said, crossly. "It will have to be sardines. Now, where did I put them... Huh?"

22

He was staring at an empty plate. All six sardines had vanished. But this time, he had a good idea who the thief was.

Alfie was furious. First, no cornflakes. Then, no eggs. Now, no sardines. He would have to make waffles.

24

Alfie set the table and turned on the oven. Then he went to get his waffles.

25

Grrr! Someone had beaten him to it. Luckily, they'd left a trail. Alfie followed it.

26

The thieves hadn't eaten the waffles. But now Alfie didn't want to eat them either.

27

Pause after page 27.

You could ask:

- What ***had*** the mice done with Alfie's waffles?
- What is there left for him to eat? Can you remember?

Suggested session 2

If you are reading the story in two sessions, you might like to go over the story so far. What do the children remember from the previous session? Look through the first part of the book to refresh their memories.

When you are ready, ask the children to read chapters 5-8 (pages 28-46) whilst you monitor and record strategies.

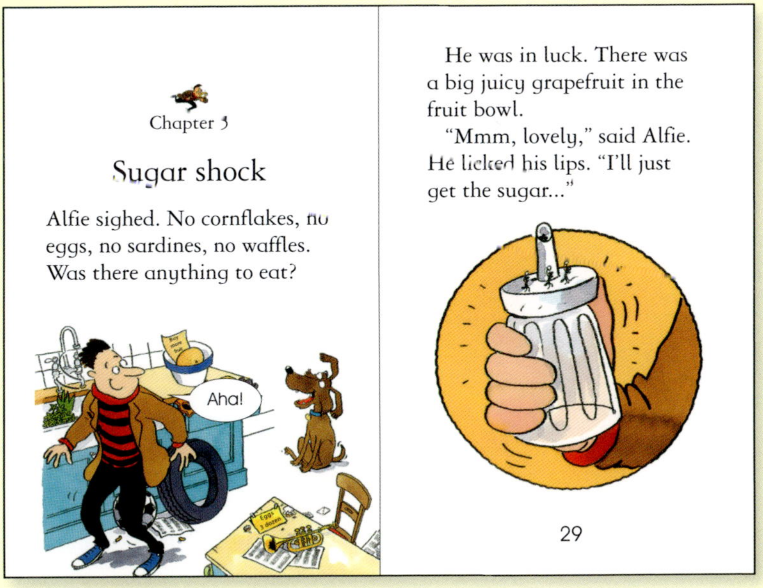
Chapter 5

Sugar shock

Alfie sighed. No cornflakes, no eggs, no sardines, no waffles. Was there anything to eat?

He was in luck. There was a big juicy grapefruit in the fruit bowl.

"Mmm, lovely," said Alfie. He licked his lips. "I'll just get the sugar..."

29

It wasn't just one sneaky creep. There were hundreds.
But they were very small.

Alfie took out his magnifying glass. He'd soon find out who was making off with his sugar.

31

Chapter 6

Still no breakfast

By the time Alfie had solved the mystery, there wasn't a single grain of sugar left.
Alfie felt hungry and very, very cross.

32

"No cornflakes, no eggs, no sardines, no waffles!" he yelled. A few seconds later, he had no grapefruit either.

Then he paused. Oh dear! Maybe this was how people felt when he burgled their houses. Alfie felt ashamed.

But he also still felt hungry. There was only one thing left to do. He would have to go out for breakfast.

34

Pause after page 34.

You could ask:

- Alfie doesn't look happy, does he?
  How is he feeling?
  Elicit the word "ashamed".
- What could he be thinking?
  You could provide speech or thought bubble notes for children to write down their ideas.

Now ask the children to read pages 35-38.

Chapter 7

Paper plan

At Rosie's Café, Alfie ate an enormous breakfast. But even that didn't cheer him up.

As he drank his coffee, Alfie glanced at a newspaper. He read something which gave him an idea.

He took a closer look.

37

NEED A JOB?

Can you:
Follow trails?
Track down stolen goods?
Catch crooks?
Spot clues?
Keep a cool head?

The STOP-A-THIEF
Detective Agency
needs
YOU!

38

Pause after page 38.

You could ask:

- Do you think Alfie would be a good detective? Why?

Now ask the children to read pages 39-45.

"Can I follow trails?" thought Alfie, remembering his trip to the park.

39

"Can I track down stolen goods?" he wondered.

"Without even trying!" he said.

40

"Can I catch crooks?" he asked himself. "I certainly can – and Tibbles won't steal my fish again!"

41

"Can I spot clues?" he said. He rubbed his chin. "Ha! I can spot clues almost invisible to the naked eye."

42

Chapter 8

A new job?

"I can do all of those things!" said Alfie. Then he read the last line of the list.

"Can I keep a cool head? Hmmm..."

43

Alfie shrugged. He hadn't been cool about the grapefruit. But who can keep their cool when they're very hungry?

44

The Stop-A-Thief Detective Agency gave Alfie a job the same day. The boss had never known anyone like him.

45

Pause after page 45.

You could ask:

- How do you think Alfie caught the burglar in the picture?

Now ask the children to read page 46.

Alfie caught more crooks in his first week than all the other detectives put together.

And he never stole another thing – not even breakfast.

46

You could ask:

- What other adventures do you think Alfie might have with the detective agency?

Now return to the text (see overleaf) to discuss whether the children's answers and predictions were correct, and talk about their approaches.

Return to the text

The return to the text allows you to reinforce teaching points, e.g. checking children's understanding, identifying and reinforcing successful decoding strategies.

Look through the story again to recap on strategies the children have used for decoding unfamiliar words (e.g. phonic, graphic, context or syntax).

You might say:

- I really liked the way (***child's name***) worked out how to read (***word or phrase***) – can you tell us how you did it?

Talk about the story as a whole.

You might ask:

- Were there any parts of the story that surprised you?
- Which part (or character or picture) did you like best?
- Did you like the ending? Can you think of a different way the story could have ended?
- Do you know any other stories like this?

Further reading

Young Reading Series One

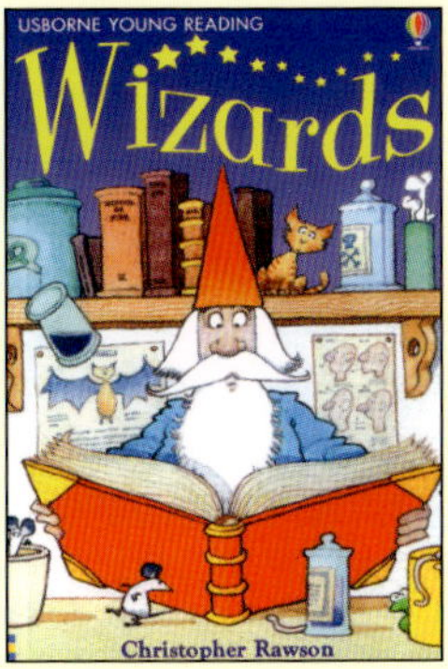

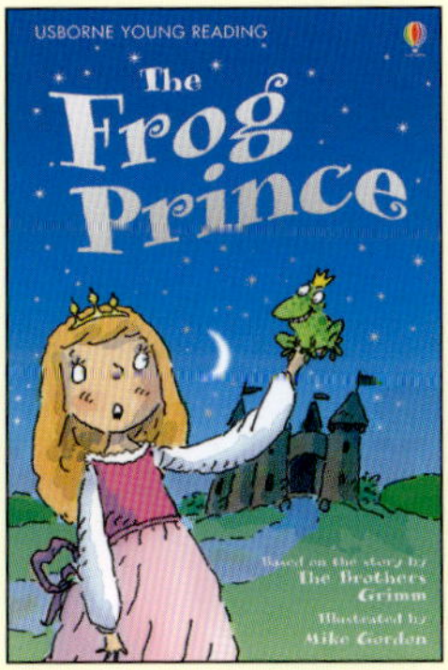

There are over 100 titles available in the Young Reading series, and more are being added all the time. To find out about all the titles available, go to **www.usborne.com**

Guided Reading Record

Text: *The Burglar's Breakfast - secure level 2*

Class:...

Group:...

Date:..

Teacher/
Teaching Assistant:...

At Level 2B, it is expected that children:

1. Can read independently and with increasing fluency on longer and less familiar texts.
2. Read whole books on their own, choosing and justifying selections.
3. Can explain their reaction to texts, commenting on important aspects.
4. Can explain organisational features including alphabetical order, layout, diagrams, captions, hyperlinks and bullet points.
5. Can draw together ideas and information from across a whole text, using simple signposts in the text.
6. Explore how particular words are used, including words and expressions with similar meanings.
7. Read medium and high frequency words automatically.

Name: Comments: Target:	Name: Comments: Target:
Name: Comments: Target:	Name: Comments: Target:
Name: Comments: Target:	Name: Comments: Target:

About the Usborne Reading Programme

The Usborne Reading Programme is a collection of over 150 titles for beginner readers, graded in seven levels from very beginners to fully confident readers. Launched in 2002, it has since sold almost 5 million copies worldwide.

The Usborne Reading Programme combines vivid, engaging writing with captivating full-colour illustration on every page. From classic tales to lively non-fiction, there is something to appeal to everyone.

From one level to the next, there is a clear progression in terms of subject, style, narrative length, sentence structure and vocabulary, giving children the satisfaction of mastering real books and making measurable progress without overstretching them and causing them to lose enthusiasm.

Non-fiction titles at all levels draw on the expertise of a range of specialists in their subject, ensuring that the books are not only engaging but authoritative: for example, Eva Schloss, stepsister of Anne Frank, advised on **Anne Frank**, and John Woolley of the Captain Cook Memorial Museum in Whitby advised on **Captain Cook**.

The Reading Programme advisers

The Reading Programme has been developed in consultation with **Alison Kelly**, a leading expert in the teaching of reading, who helped to draw up the seven-level framework (see pages 36-37). Alison worked for many years as a primary school teacher in London, and is currently a Senior Lecturer in Education at Roehampton University, teaching about all aspects of literacy.

Suzanne Maile is assistant headteacher at Sheen Mount Primary School in south-west London, a thriving school with a reputation for outstanding teaching and learning. Suzanne is responsible for curriculum development and initial teacher training at Sheen Mount, and has extensive experience in teaching guided reading at all levels. She is also a teacher tutor at Roehampton University, and a consultant teacher for Richmond LEA.

Alison and Suzanne have chosen a selection of titles from the Reading Programme that are particularly suitable for guided reading, and produced comprehensive teacher's notes packed with ideas and guidance for guided reading sessions.
The range of titles in the Reading Programme provides wide scope for further reading at every level.

The Usborne Reading Programme and the National Curriculum

The Usborne Reading Progamme is fully integrated with the National Curriculum for English at Key Stages 1 and 2, encouraging children to develop fluent and accurate reading across a range of texts, subjects and styles.

Selected titles from all levels of the Reading Programme are available as Guided Reading packs, comprising six copies of the book plus comprehensive teacher's notes. Guided Reading packs represent a selection of text types, and are carefully graded within levels 1-4 of the National Curriculum.

Text type: European folktale
NC level: 1C

Text type: Asian folktale
NC level: 1B

Text type: adapted children's classic
NC level: 1A

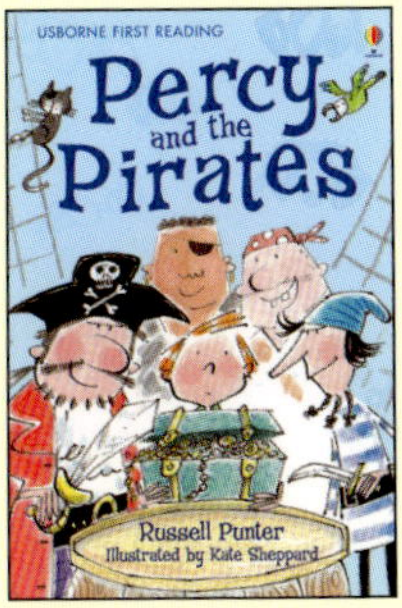

Text type:
original fiction
NC level: 2C

Text type:
original fiction
NC level: 2B

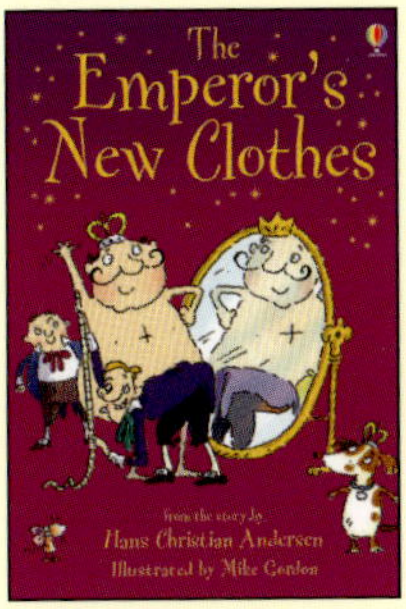

Text type:
classic fairytale
NC level: 2A

Text type:
myths and legends
NC level: 3C

Text type: adapted children's classic
NC level: 3B

Text type:
adapted classic
NC level: 3A

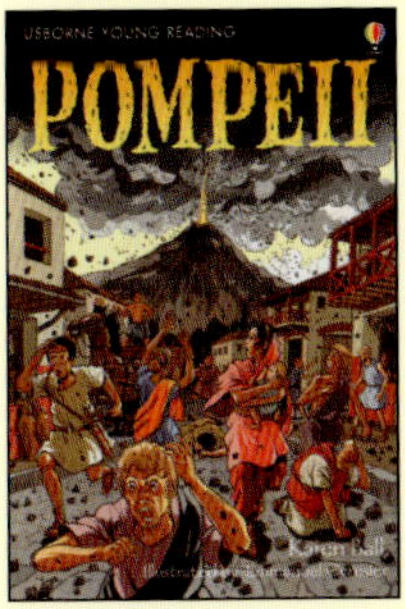

Text type:
non-fiction (history)
NC level: 4C

Text type:
biography
NC level: 4B

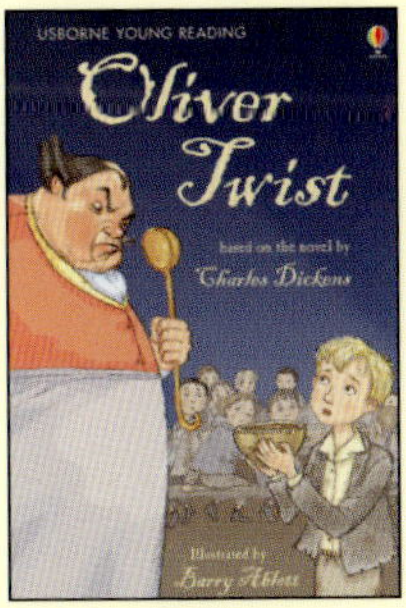

Text type:
adapted classic
NC level: 4A

The Usborne Reading

	Number of words	Themes
First Reading Level One National Curriculum level 1	up to 150	Classic tales (e.g. Aesop's Fables) and folktales
First Reading Level Two National Curriculum level 1	up to 250	As Level One, including less familiar folktales
First Reading Level Three National Curriculum level 1-2	up to 450	As Level Two plus original fiction and non-fiction (natural history life cycles)
First Reading Level Four National Curriculum level 2	up to 750	As Level Three plus classic fairy tales
Young Reading Series One National Curriculum level 2-3	1,000-1,500	Fairy tales, fantasy, fiction, non-fiction ("the story of...")
Young Reading Series Two National Curriculum level 3	2,000-2,500	As Series One plus adapted classics
Young Reading Series Three National Curriculum level 3-4	4,000-5,000	History, biographies, classics

The elements above are intended as guidelines only, and whilst distinctions between different levels remain clear,

Programme framework

Content	Vocabulary
Short single narrative followed by reading and comprehension puzzles	Simple everyday vocabulary, familiar items
Single narrative plus character sheets and/or maps, and puzzles	More descriptive and evocative vocabulary, always clear in context
Single narrative with repeated elements, plus character sheets and/or maps, no puzzles	Powerful verbs and adjectives, clear in context
Single narrative	More exotic elements and controlled use of idiom
Several linked stories or one longer narrative in chapters. Direct and indirect speech, intertextual references	Wide-ranging everyday vocabulary
Single narrative in chapters. Introduce irony and subplot, allow opportunity for inference and deduction	More challenging, building on Series One; specialist or technical terms explained
Single narrative in chapters. Assumes some relevant background knowledge	Building on Series Two, may assume knowledge of specialist or technical terms

exceptions may sometimes be made to individual specifications in the interests of narrative or style.

Notes

On The Edge

by Susan Price

On The Edge

by Susan Price

CONTENTS

TRUFFLE

Martin's throat was hoarse with the cold air, and with calling. The end of his nose and the tips of his ears stung with cold. His fingers were numb, as were his toes inside his trainers, but he *must* find Truffle.

It was as though he'd made a bargain: if I suffer – get really cold, frostbite, and my nose drops off – then I'll have paid what it costs to find Truffle.

He'd imagined it would be a simple matter. A walk round the lanes and through the woods, a few shouts – and Truffle would come running, his tongue lolling out of his laughing mouth, his tail wagging.

"He's run away for good this time," his mother had commented. "He won't be back."

Martin hadn't taken much notice. Truffle had gone missing previously – for nearly three days once – and he'd always re-emerged. His mother always expected the worst. She enjoyed being pessimistic, that's what his Dad said.

Martin was determined to locate Truffle, and prove her wrong. She was wrong about a heap of things. His dad would return. Truffle would return. They'd all live together once more, and things would be happier.

For hours and hours he'd searched up and down the village lanes, climbing banks into the woods and fields. And calling. Annie and Jessie had come along to help.

Around noon, the girls had said they were returning home, and he'd accompanied them to Annie's house. Her mother had served them all fish fingers and mugs of hot chocolate. Then he'd noticed that it was nearly two o'clock. "I've got to go," he said. The girls had refused to accompany him in such freezing conditions.

He'd tramped round the lanes again, calling, until he met Joe, Dan and Mike. "You seen my dog?"

They hadn't but were happy to join him. Together they trudged up the long, snowy drives to two farmhouses, knocking at the doors and asking permission to search the farmyards.

"Don't fret," said one farmer. "He'll be back when he's hungry." Then Joe and Dan lost interest, and all of them went off and made a slide on the steep hill at one end of the village. The running and sliding warmed them thoroughly. Martin was taken aback when Mike said, "I'm going in. Time for me tea," and the others agreed. He hadn't realised it was so late – or so dark. And he still hadn't located Truffle.

He hadn't even been searching. He'd been playing. That made him feel guilty. He watched the others wandering off through the dark and thought: I'm not going in until I find him.

He'd searched all round the village several times without any luck. It was time to rethink.

Where could Truffle be?

Maybe he was at Uncle Joe's.

Truffle had been born at Uncle Joe's. His mother, Prissy, belonged to Uncle Joe, and Martin, his mum and dad and Truffle had all walked over to Uncle Joe's no end of times. Well, often enough for Truffle to know the way.

It wasn't that far to Uncle Joe's. He could easily walk there before it got really late.

Uncle Joe and Auntie Mags would have to put him up for the night if he walked over there and got his shoes soaked through in the snow. He'd get to spend the night with his cousin Pete, sharing a room. Auntie Mags always had biscuits in a tin. The idea seemed better and better. He might even see his dad. Uncle Joe was his dad's brother.

It was pointless going home first. His mother would prevent him going. She didn't really care about Truffle being missing. Having made up his mind, he felt better. Down the hill he went, through the village, past the pub and the newer houses, and up the steep hill towards the woods. His feet made no sound on the icy road. He was hot inside his coat, though his fingers and toes were cold. They'll warm up, he thought, and felt that he was achieving something. He was finding Truffle.

He remembered the place where you had to turn off the road and into the woods perfectly. There was a hedge to clamber through. His trainers got filled with snow, and his jeans were soaked almost to his knees. Never mind: a bit of snow never killed anybody.

Now he had to follow the track that led through the trees, and climb the steep Edge to the top. He felt quite proud of himself for remembering the way. His mother would be so surprised, and impressed, when he came home with Truffle. "I told you I'd find him," he'd say, and if his dad phoned, he could tell him how he'd guessed where Truffle would be, and how he had walked all the way to Uncle Joc's and fetched him back. His dad would be impressed too. And proud. He might even come over and see them, and they could tidy the house, him and his mum, and his dad would want to remain.

The path zig-zagged up the steep side of the Edge. No snow lay on the path but the ground was frozen and slippery. After slogging up the hill for a bit Martin paused, undecided. It didn't seem such an easy walk to Uncle Joe's now. Maybe it hadn't been such a great idea. Maybe he should go home, and take up the search again tomorrow.

It was further than he usually walked by himself, without his dad to urge him on. But his dad wasn't going to be around much, was he? He'd just have to urge himself on. If he got cold and tired – well, that would just show that he was serious about finding Truffle.

It might be a good idea to take the shortest way and not hang around. So he left the path and plunged into the snow that lay deep on the hillside. The snow dragged at his legs and made the climb twice as hard. He stumbled, went sprawling face down in the snow, and laughed as he scrambled to his feet. Clambering on uphill, he ducked under a snow-laden tree, which dumped its load on him. Snow soaked his hair and fell down inside his jacket.

He was wet, but not cold – the exercise made him glow. Refusing to rest, panting, sweating, he slogged on.

When he reached the top, he had a stitch and his lungs hurt. As he gasped, clouds of steam came from his mouth. He opened his jacket. He was perspiring so much that he spread his arms and stood in the strong wind that blew up there on the hilltop, letting his jacket blow out behind him. He stood flapping his arms and gazing at the stars until he realised he was shivering.

His clothes were wet with snow and sweat, and the cold wind cut straight through them. He was more than cooled – he was chilled. He tried to fasten his jacket, but the zip had gone wonky again. It just wouldn't zip up. The wind kept catching his jacket and blowing it wide, until his teeth were chattering. Clacketty-clack, they went, if he didn't hold his jaw tight.

He'd be warmer once he got off the top of the hill. The path he needed to take was just a bit further along the hill-top.

He walked along the hill, trying to hold his jacket round himself. Below him was darkness. At a distance, the light from a house glimmered, but there weren't many houses around the Edge. Peering down into that darkness, he felt like the only person in the world, and he realised how far he still had to walk. For a moment, he felt scared – but then he was excited. He would do it. He'd walk all the way, in the dark, on his own – an adventure. Imagine the look on Uncle Joe and Auntie Mags' faces when they opened the door to find him standing there in the dark!

He wandered along the hillside, searching for the path he recollected, and moving his chilled limbs clumsily. He could barely keep his jacket around him.

Thoughts of going home recurred. He was hungry, cold and wet. No, it would be cowardly to back out now. Just keep going, he told himself. Arctic explorers have to. They grit their teeth and battle on, into the teeth of the wind.

He found the path and set off down it. The wind dropped, which brought relief. It was difficult to see where he was putting his feet in the dark, but the path was wide, and he walked briskly.

Now the path split into three different ways. He didn't remember it doing that. Which way to go? He decided that straight on was probably best.

There was no one else about – no one he could see, anyway – and the woods were silent. Snow silent. Dark and silent. He tried not to think of werewolves. There weren't any wolves in Britain. How about werefoxes then? Werebadgers? He tried to laugh, but the thoughts didn't amuse him. If anything, they frightened him even more. Then he realised that the path was going the wrong way.

He stood still, to think. It wasn't easy to think because of the shivering – shivering, shivering, all the time. Even when he tried to hold himself still, he couldn't. Every now and again, an especially big shiver would make his teeth clatter.

Was the path going in the wrong direction? He wasn't sure. All the different ways looked the same. He thought

Uncle Joe's was over that way ... But how was he to tell?

He didn't know where he was.

He was suddenly terrified of the darkness all round him, the silence, the cold, the long empty miles between him and home. He desperately wanted someone to come and help him, but no one knew where he was.

"I'm cold!" he said to the darkness and the trees. No one, nothing, answered.

A noise, a rustling, focused his mind. Something was moving in the dark, close by him, crackling among the frozen twigs. He longed to run, but his freezing legs wouldn't budge.

A darkness moved on the path, drew closer to him – and snuffled at his hand. He saw an eye gleam, and suddenly the darkness made sense – a tail was waving.

"Truffle!" He tried to crouch, but was too stiff with cold. He fell to his knees, hugging the dog. Truffle shoved against him, snuffled in his ear, licked his cheek. "Where've you been, you stupid dog? Have you been at Uncle Joe's? Have you?"

Truffle pulled free of him, trotted ahead on the path and looked back.

Martin, rising, started to follow. "D'you know the way? Show me the way, then – good boy!"

It was hard to see Truffle in the dark – he was mostly brown, with only a little bib of white on his chest. Twice, Martin thought the dog had left him, and he was lost again, but at his call, Truffle came running back up the path, jumping up at him and wagging his tail before running on in front again. After the first couple of times, Martin knew that Truffle wasn't going to abandon him.

Truffle led him downhill, always downhill, sometimes by paths and sometimes through bushes. They came out from trees and onto a road. Truffle ran ahead, his paws pattering on the frost.

When Martin saw the narrow, hump-backed bridge, he gave a shout. "I know where we are now!" He tried to run, to lead the way, but he could only hobble. Still, he hobbled to the top of the bridge, and from there he saw the street where Uncle Joe lived. "Come on, Truff!"

Despite the cold, and the pain of his numb hands and feet, Martin felt proud and delighted as he knocked on Uncle Joe's door. He'd reached here, all by himself, and he'd found Truffle too. Everyone would be impressed.

Uncle Joe opened the door. He looked amazed, even more amazed than Martin had hoped. Then he grabbed Martin by the shoulder and pulled him indoors, shouting, "Mags! Here's Martin! Soaking wet and half-froze! Get on the phone to Lisa, quick!"

As Martin stumbled into the hallway, his uncle was reaching to shut the door. "No – wait! Wait for Truffle!"

"Truffle?" asked his uncle.

"Truffle's behind me." Martin pulled the door open again and stood on the step, looking about. Truffle wasn't in the small front garden, or on the street. Martin yelled for him, and waited for him to come running.

Uncle Joe said quietly, "You go in to your auntie and get warm, and I'll wait for Truffle."

Auntie Mags appeared in the hallway saying, "Martin!

Come and tell your mother you're all right." Martin staggered clumsily down the hall to her, still shivering. She caught hold of his hands, and pressed her own warm hand to his cheek. "No, hot shower first," she said. "Upstairs you go!"

"I'll phone his mother," Uncle Joe said, coming down the hall. He'd shut the front door.

"Where's Truffle?" Martin asked.

"Never mind Truffle for now," Auntie Mags said gently. "Come on, I'll find you a towel."

After the shower, Martin felt almost normal again, and Auntie Mags gave him some dry clothes of Peter's. She'd warmed them on a radiator. He went downstairs and sat by the fire with Uncle Joe. Truffle wasn't there. He supposed he was in the kitchen with Auntie Mags.

"Where's Peter?" Martin asked.

"Over his friend's. What were you doing, wandering about on a night like this?"

"I was looking for Truffle," Martin said.

"Look at your clothes," Uncle Joe said. "Denim. Cotton. No warmth in it once it gets wet. You lose all your body heat. It can kill you."

"I found Truffle," Martin said.

Auntie Mags came in with a mug and a sandwich on a plate. Martin looked round, expecting Truffle to follow her in. Old Prissy came stumping along, and snuffed at his hand in greeting. "Is Truffle still eating?" Martin asked.

Auntie Mags gave him the mug and put the plate on the arm of the sofa. "Truffle isn't here, Martin."

Martin, surprised, looked at his uncle. "Why didn't you let him in?"

"It wasn't Truffle, Martin," Uncle Joe said. "It must have been some other dog."

"It was Truffle!" As if he didn't know his own dog! "He showed me the way here!"

His uncle and aunt exchanged glances, and then looked away. They said nothing for a long time. Martin sensed something was wrong. What, he didn't know.

"Your mother's coming over to fetch you," Uncle Joe said at last. "She's getting a neighbour to give her a lift. She's been concerned."

"You're welcome here any time," Auntie Mags said, "but you should tell your mother before you come."

"And you should have more sense than to walk here in weather like this," Uncle Joe said.

Martin didn't like that. He thought that he and Truffle should be praised, not told off. And Uncle Joe had no right to shut Truffle out. Sulking, Martin drank his hot chocolate, and when Auntie Mags tried to talk – about school, as if he wanted to talk about school anyway – he wouldn't answer except for "yes" or "no" when he absolutely had to say something.

Then there was a hammering at the door, and his mother had arrived. That was all he needed.

In she came, shouting, "Oh, I've been so worried, I've been frantic!"

Well, she hadn't been too worried about Truffle, had she?

"Oh, Joe, Mags, I can't thank you enough – "

They didn't do anything, Martin thought. It was Truffle who rescued me.

"Martin, haven't you got anything to say?"

"Where's Truffle?" Martin asked. "Have *you* left him outside as well?"

His mother went very quiet and still. So did Uncle Joe and Auntie Mags.

"We didn't tell him," Aunt Mags said.

"We thought you should do that," said Uncle Joe, his arms folded.

"Tell me what?" Martin asked.

From her coat pocket, Martin's mother took something, and handed it to him. It was Truffle's worn red collar.

“I couldn’t tell you,” she said. “I thought, what with everything, you’d be so upset ...”

“Tell me what?” Martin asked.

Uncle Joe unfolded his arms. “Truffle was run over last night, Martin. I’m sorry, but – Truffle is dead.”

THE CLIFF EDGE

I blame my dad. He taught us how to trespass. He taught us how to wriggle under barbed wire fences without getting caught up on them, and how to tell by the bird-calls whether someone was coming. Notices that read TRESPASSERS WILL BE PROSECUTED might as well have said COME ON IN.

My dad would put my brother, sister and me in the car, drive us out to the country, and say, "Off you go."

And off we'd go, for hours, while Dad pottered round by himself, bird-watching. We'd wander through forests of fern higher than our heads, climb trees, dam streams, walk for miles.

One time, when I was feeling out of sorts with my brother and sister, I went off on my own. I let them run on ahead and then took another path. I wasn't worried about them. They were as familiar with the woods as I was, and they'd go back to the car by themselves when they were ready.

I enjoyed being by myself for a change. I climbed the steep hill known as "The Edge", and came to a forestry plantation with a barbed wire fence round it, and notices saying, NO TRESPASSING. I peered into the deeps of this pine forest, and felt a romantic shiver about wild, lonely woods. So I wriggled backwards under the barbed wire.

It was much darker beneath the trees. They were all stiff, thin pine trees with deep, dark green needles that seemed to suck the light out of the air. I strode along a straight, broad pathway through the trees, while ahead of me the trees faded into blurry darkness. It was the same when I checked behind. The pine scent was strong, the silence deep.

I was soon bored with walking on this wide path, and turned off into the trees. The ground was inches deep in old needles and it was soft and springy.

The terrain sloped steeply downwards. At first I wasn't bothered, but it got gradually steeper, until it was hard to stand upright. The trees continued down and across the hillside, in long parallel lines.

I expected to reach the bottom of the hill fairly soon, but still the slope carried on. I decided there was no point in descending all the way to the bottom, when I would have to climb all the way back up again.

I turned and started to climb up. At my first step a great wodge of pine needles slid away under my foot, and I went sprawling, sliding down the slope on my side. It was a gentle, slow slide, but when I tried to get to my feet, I slid faster. Down and down I went, past tree after tree. I couldn't stand and I couldn't stop.

I laughed. It was pleasant to skim down the slope, like sledging without snow or sledge. Then the slope levelled out a bit, and that brought me to a stop. I thought, now I've got even further to climb. And it was getting darker. I'd better get going.

As soon as I took a step, the pine needles slid away, and down I went again. *Wheee!* This is fun, I thought. I might as well go all the way down to the bottom, and enjoy it. But where was the bottom? I peered ahead through the dusk and the trees, but the slope seemed endless.

There was something odd about what was in front of me. I squinted, trying to see in the dark. The lines of trees in front of me seemed twisted.

You know how, when you put a pencil into a glass of water, the pencil looks bent, even though it's straight? It was rather like that. There were tall straight trees all around me and ahead of me – but somehow, in the distance, the trees seemed bent, twisted. I kept trying to see how or why, but everything was so grey and blurry that I couldn't make it out.

I caught at a sapling that I happened to be passing, and clambered back up the slope, on all fours, because it was so steep. I was very careful and managed three steps before the mat of pine needles slipped away. I laughed as I went sliding down the slope again. It seemed so funny at the time.

But the trees ahead of me, further down the slope, still had that peculiar bentness. Well, I thought, I'll find out what's wrong with them when I get down there. And *wheee!* – here I go.

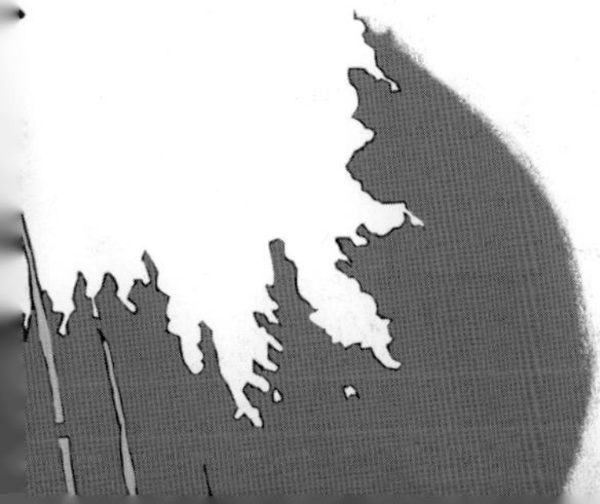

But then – as I was still sliding down the hill – I thought about what a long time it was going to take me to get back to the car. What if I couldn't climb the slope at all, but had to walk all the way round the bottom of the hill? It would take all night. Everyone would be waiting for me. They'd be really angry when I finally turned up. I'd be in real trouble. Perhaps I'd better climb back to the top after all. And be really careful this time.

The bentness of the trees in front of me looked odder and odder too. Even the light was different, down there. It was brighter. How could that be?

There was a tree in front of me, a little to one side. It wasn't very big, but big enough to stop me. I angled myself as I slid, so that one of my feet hit the tree, and I stopped sliding.

I lay there for a while, with my foot braced against the pine tree. I stared at what was in front of me, trying to make sense of it. My brain told me there were more tall pine trees, going on down a slope in straight lines, and I frowned as I tried to see that. It wasn't what my eyes were seeing. There was a struggle between my eyes and my brain. Then it snapped into focus. I saw what was really in front of me.

The slope I'd been sliding down ended half a metre

beyond the tree I had my foot braced against. Just ended. Stopped.

Beyond that were the tops of tall pine trees growing far below. That was why they'd seemed twisted out of true. They weren't tall, straight trunks going down a slope. They were tall pointed tops rising up from below. A long way below, because those pine trees were tall.

And that was why there was more light down there. It wasn't a slope shadowed by trees. It was wide open air above the tree-tops.

It seemed to take a long time for what this meant to work its way into my brain. I'd been enjoying sliding down the slope. I'd been laughing and planning to slide all the way to the bottom. *Wheee!* – what fun! If I'd slid half a metre further, I'd have shot straight over the edge. I'd have fallen – how far? Down I'd have gone, down into the tops of those trees, crashing through the thin upper branches, bashed against the thicker ones, breaking my ribs – and on and on, down and down, to the ground. Would I still have been alive when I hit the ground?

I could feel myself falling as I lay with my foot against the tree. I felt the upward lurch of my heart and guts. I felt the cold wind rush around me as I hurtled down – flying to a crash landing.

Maybe I would have survived, but I would have been all broken up. I trembled with relief. Thank goodness I'd been curious about why the trees looked odd; thank goodness I'd been too idle to want to climb all the way back to the top. Thank goodness I'd seen that tree within reach and stuck out my foot.

Then, like a smack round the face, I realised that I was still half a metre from the cliff edge, and every time I'd tried to take a step up the slope, the pine needles had slid away. If I tried to move from here, it would happen again.

And this time, I had no space to spare. The very first time I slipped, I would go over the edge.

I looked over my shoulder. I couldn't see the top of the slope for the darkness between the trees. It was very, very steep. I lay with my foot against the tree trunk, afraid to move. Maybe, I thought, if I stay here and keep still, someone will come and rescue me.

When? It might be hours before Dad worried and started looking for me. Even then, no one would think to look for me here. No one came here for days at a time. Search helicopters wouldn't see me through the trees.

Soon it would be full dark. I'd get cold. What if I got cramp? What if I fell asleep? I'd go over the edge, and no one might ever know what happened to me. This seemed dreadful, almost worse than being killed.

It was no use hoping to be rescued. You got yourself into this, I told myself. You have to get yourself out.

I looked round. I knew that I had to make absolutely certain I didn't slip with my first step, because I had no room to risk it.

I brought my other foot onto the tree that was holding me back from the edge. Then I peered round in the grey dusk.

There was a big tree root, poking out from the pine needles. It was a thick, strong root because it was holding the tree on the very edge of the cliff. The root was actually closer to the edge than I was, and I was scared of going any closer. But it was the strongest, most solid looking foothold I could see. It took me a long time to nerve myself to do it, but then I slid myself a little closer to the edge, and wedged my feet firmly against the root. Now I was right above that drop. I felt myself tipping into it, and the hair moved in my scalp. A voice in me said, "Why not just throw yourself into that empty air and get it over with?"

Sick with fear, I reached out for the spreading branches of a tree growing higher up the slope. I filled my hands with the tough, prickly branches before I dared to take an upwards step.

I dug my foot into the depths of pine needles, trying to ensure that I was resting on the firm ground beneath them all. When I thought I could feel the ground, I put my weight on that foot, while keeping tight hold of the pine branches. I hoped that, if I did slip, my hold on the branches would save me from going over the edge. In my mind I could imagine the branches tearing through my hands as I went over anyway.

That first step held. I took another, hauling on the branches, and got hold of the tree's trunk. I hugged it and leaned against it. Two steps away from the edge! I peered through the dusk for my next safe move.

There was a darker patch on the slope near me. I guessed it was a hollow or a ledge. Uneven ground like that had stopped my slide down the slope earlier. If I could step onto that ledge, and it held me, I could reach the next tree. So here goes.

I took a step and my foot slipped. I brought up my other foot and lunged, grabbing with my hands for the ledge – and thankfully, I'd been right. It *was* a ledge, and I scrambled onto it. I lay there, curled up, my heart thumping, until I felt brave enough to stand up and grab for the nearest tree.

It was getting steadily darker, everything turning dark grey. It was harder and harder to see the roots and ledges that would give me a safe foothold. I comforted myself with thinking that I had, at least, managed to get further up the slope. If I did slip, I had more chance of saving myself.

I thought out and planned every little movement of foot and hand on that long, slow climb to the top of the slope. Every time I embraced a tall, solid tree trunk, there was a little blaze of triumph. Still safe!

Gradually, as I got higher, the slope became less steep, and even if I did slip a little – as I did – I didn't toboggan away down the hill. By the time I reached the top, it was so dark that I could hardly pick out the trees. I made my way through them to the broad path that I wished I'd never left, and I ran out onto it with a whoop of relief. Scared wood pigeons rose up with a clatter of wings.

I fairly danced along the path. I was so glad not to be lying in pieces at the bottom of the cliff. I'd got myself into a stupid fix, but nobody need find out about it, because I'd got myself out of it too. I could have panicked and frozen, and still be lying there with one foot against the tree, too terrified to move. I could have lost my reason and gone over the edge. But I hadn't done either. I'd kept my head, and saved myself. I was delighted, exhilarated.

It was tricky finding my way back to the car. In the dark, everything looks different. I wandered onto the wrong paths, went round in circles and cracked my head on branches I couldn't see, but I got there in the end.

"So you've decided to show up at last," Dad said, but he didn't seem all that put out, so I couldn't have kept him waiting much longer than usual. I thought I'd been away for hours, but maybe it had been much less.

I didn't say anything to anyone about what had happened until years later, though I thought about it a lot.

I thought about it when I had to go up on stage in front of the whole school, or when I was called to the Head's office for skipping lessons, or when a bigger girl threatened to get me on the way home. Who cares? I'd think. You kept your head and saved yourself from the cliff edge and that was really scary. You can deal with a little thing like this. And I did, more or less. I coped with some things better than others, but I survived.

It did wonders for me, the cliff edge. I'm glad I didn't go over it but now I'm glad that I nearly did.

Jennifer Appleby

She'd allowed plenty of time for them to be gone. When school finished, she dawdled behind everyone, ducked into the toilets, locked herself into a cubicle and waited until the din had died down in the corridors. By the time she'd come out, the school was empty and silent.

Even so, she'd taken her time, wandering round the empty corridors, looking at the paintings and reading the notices on the notice-boards, even though they were boring. She'd left the building by a door she didn't usually take, and had walked all round the school to reach her road home. By then she was nearly half-an-hour behind everyone else, so with a bit of luck she'd be safe.

But they enjoyed making her life miserable so much that they'd waited for her.

There was a little park that she walked through on her way home, and they were lingering. It made sense, because no one was about. When she saw them, she thought: I certainly won't come this way tomorrow. Of course, she still had to get through the next few moments.

She didn't know why they picked on her. She hadn't done anything to them. What had they got against her?

"Here we are at last," said Donna. She was a thin, pretty blonde girl, the leader. "Where've you been?"

Kayleigh, the big one, her arms folded, said, "You've kept us waiting."

"Tch, tch, tch," said Lesley, shaking her head.

Jen, hooking her thumbs through the straps of her rucksack, made to walk by, ignoring them. Once or twice she'd got away with ignoring them.

Kayleigh grabbed hold of the rucksack straps and hauled her back, tugging the strap from Jen's shoulders. The others came and joined in. Jen was surrounded, mobbed.

"Get it off her!" They pulled her arms behind her, dragging the rucksack from her shoulders.

Jen shrugged out of it and stood to one side, watching as they stood, laughing, holding her rucksack between them. They opened it. Jen said nothing. She knew it would be a waste of energy. If she tried to intervene, the three of them would push her away. If she waited, she might, eventually, be able to pick up her things and make off. She was sick with shame, but she'd tried fighting back and it hadn't done her any good.

Donna read one of Jen's exercise books. "That's not very good, is it? You've got to try harder!" She threw the book at Jen, who turned her head aside. Even so, it clipped the side of her face before falling to the gravel.

"D'you think she's got love-letters in here?" Kayleigh asked. "Have you? Got love-letters?"

"Not her," Donna said. "Who'd be interested in her?"

Books fell to the ground as they took them from the bag and dropped them. A green pencil case was dropped and then kicked, by Lesley, as far as she could across the grass.

"Now go and fetch that back."

There was a stranger with them.

"I said, go and fetch that back."

The three girls stopped rummaging in Jen's bag and looked round.

A woman stood near them, a young woman, in a short, smart black suit and black, high-heeled boots. In one hand she carried a black briefcase. She had a polished, groomed look that was intimidating. She was Authority. Trouble. Even Jen felt alarmed, as if this woman had appeared to dole out punishment.

Looking straight at Donna, the woman said, patiently, but with an edge to her voice, as if she was going to lose her temper very shortly: "Go and fetch the pencil case back."

"Why should I?" Donna answered. "It wasn't me."

Donna's voice was pitched a little too high and too sharp. Jen would have laughed, if she'd dared. Donna was scared of the woman.

"Go – and – fetch – it – back," the woman repeated, staring steadily at Donna.

Donna shifted uneasily, as if she might be about to take a step.

Jen didn't know what to think. It was so good, to see the bullies ordered about. It scared her, though, since she was very sure they would make her pay for it at some later date.

Lesley said, "I'll get it. It was me that kicked it."

Maybe, Jen thought, she too was afraid of getting into trouble with Donna later.

Lesley walked across the grass and picked up the pencil-case, while the other two held the rucksack between them and resentfully eyed the woman.

Lesley came back with the pencil case in her hand, and approached the woman, as if to give it to her.

The woman said, as if speaking to an idiot, "Put it back in the bag."

Lesley changed direction to do as she was told, keeping her head bowed, to hide her face.

"Now pick the other things up and put them away," the woman said. Lesley stooped to obey at once. "All of you," said the woman.

"Why – ?" Donna started.

"Just do it, Donna," the woman said.

The shock of discovering that the woman knew her name made Donna crouch and start picking up books, along with the others.

The woman stepped nearer and stood over them. "Donna Mills," she said. "Kayleigh Cunningham. Lesley White. Yes," she said, as they looked up, startled. "I know your names. I know where you live. I know your parents. Do they know what nasty, spiteful pieces of work you are?"

Everything had been put back in the bag. The three girls stood up and Donna, holding the rucksack, offered it timidly to the woman.

"It's not mine," she said, and nodded to Jen. "Give it back to Jennifer. And apologise."

Jen hadn't recovered from the shock of hearing that the woman knew her name too, when there was Donna in front of her, handing her the rucksack back.

"Sorry," Donna muttered, and hurried past.

"Sorry," said Lesley, passing her with head lowered. Kayleigh just hurried after the others, without saying anything.

Jen was left alone with the woman. For a long, embarrassing while, she couldn't think of anything to say. Then she said, "Thank you."

The woman shook her head slightly, dismissing the thanks. "Do you want a lift home? You don't want to catch up with them."

Jen did want a lift home. To be carried past Donna and her friends, safely inside a car, would be pure happiness and relief, while it lasted. But this woman was a stranger. She must never accept lifts from strangers.

"I know your mother," the woman said. "She won't mind your having a lift from me."

Jen looked at the woman's face again, stared at it. She did seem faintly familiar – but Jen could remember her mother saying, "Don't get in a car with a stranger, even if they say they know me: even if they say I've sent them to fetch you."

The woman could see Jen's nervousness. "Let's go and sit down over there," she said, and walked towards a bench. Jen followed.

Seating herself, the woman took a small mobile phone from her pocket, and held it out to Jen. "Dial your mother's number, and I'll speak to her. Or do you have a phone? Perhaps you'd prefer to use your own."

Jen took the woman's phone. She'd had one of her own, but Donna, Kayleigh and Lesley had snatched it the week before, and she hadn't told her mother yet. She dreaded the row when she did. "Why did you let them take it? Am I supposed to pay their bills?" She'd got trouble at school and trouble at home.

Sitting down beside the woman on the bench, she dialled her mother's number. Before it was answered, the woman took the phone from her, and put it to her ear.

"Hello!" the woman said into the phone. "It's me. I'll be round in a few minutes, okay?"

As Jen sat astonished, the woman handed her the phone. "Speak to her."

Jen put the phone to her ear. "Hello?"

"Hello, love," said her mother's voice. "Can't wait to see you! Chockie bickies! See you!" And her mother rang off.

Jen frowned. It had been her mother's number, and her mother's voice, but it was unlike her mother to sound so enthusiastic about seeing her after an ordinary day at school.

Jen handed the phone back to the woman, and stared

at her. "Did Mum send you to fetch me?" But her mother didn't know about the bullies. She hadn't told her.

"They make your life a misery, don't they?" the woman said.

Jen looked away. She couldn't speak.

"I know," the woman said. "I went through it too."

"Every day they wait for me. They throw my books about and make a mess of them, so I get into trouble. They take my money and they took my phone. They wait for me on the way to school, and at break, and on the way home."

"What have they got against you?" the woman asked.

Jen sat quietly for a moment or two. She'd been asking herself that question over and over. "I'm just the sort of person other people don't like." She looked at the woman, who didn't say anything, but was plainly listening. "They can get away with picking on me," Jen said, "because I don't have any friends, really. And I was thinking, well, why don't I have any friends, when everybody else does? And it just came to me – I'm not likeable."

"Why not?" the woman asked.

"Well, if I was, I'd have friends. Look at me. I'm ugly.

And I'm boring. I'm only interested in boring things."

"Boring things?"

"Well, things other people think are boring. So there's nothing about me to like."

A small part of her hoped the woman would contradict her, and say that she wasn't at all boring or ugly.

"So, are you going to do something about it?" the woman enquired.

Jen was quiet again, turning her secret plan over in her mind. Well, it wasn't really a plan. She had nowhere to run to ...

The woman waited, leaning forward a little, looking at Jen, but saying nothing.

"What's the point?" Jen said, at last.

"Have you tried?" the woman asked.

"Yes, I've tried! I've tried lots of times. Nobody wants to be friends with me. Well, I wouldn't want to be friends with some boring freak everybody laughed at – who would? And when I'm grown-up, I'll still be on my own. I'm never going to get married or have a family. So it'll just be year after year of getting up, going out, being laughed at, being on my own, coming home, being on my own, going to bed, getting up ... I'd rather be dead."

"I think I would too," the woman agreed.

"So. I think ... " Jen struggled hard not to cry ... "I'll run away. I'll sleep out in the streets and freeze to death. People do freeze to death, don't they, even in this country?"

The woman looked at her steadily, and then said, "Do you think Donna and her friends would be sorry when you were dead?"

Jennifer looked down at the gravel path.

"The only people you'd make sorry would be the people you don't want to hurt – your mum and dad. Donna and the rest would throw a party."

"I don't care," Jen said.

"Very selfish," said the woman. "I nearly ran away once. I had my bag packed and everything. Had it all planned. Well ... I didn't, to be honest. My idea of a plan was to catch the first bus that came along and stay on it to wherever it went. I didn't have a clue where I was going to

sleep, or how I was going to eat. And you don't either, do you?"

Jen didn't want to answer but, after a few moments, shook her head.

"I saw sense before I did anything," the woman said. "I realised that I'd only be adding to my problems, not solving them. I thought: there's got to be something else I can do."

"There isn't though," Jen said.

"Oh, come on. Have you told your mum what's going on?"

"It's no good talking to her. I told her ages ago, when it was only just starting. She said, if she came into school and complained, it'd only make things worse. "Learn to stand up for yourself," she said, "and fight your own battles." Then she said, "But don't you get into trouble at school." How am I supposed to stand up for myself without getting into trouble? There was this girl last year. Some other girls had been picking on her, and she turned round and thumped 'em. And she got into trouble for fighting! Not the bullies! Her!"

"My mother was just the same," the woman said. "But I thought schools were keen to stop bullying these days?"

"Ha!" Jen said.

"Ah."

"They say they are. But it's all talk." Jen looked round the park. "There're no teachers here, are there? They shoot off home in their cars."

"All the same," the woman said, "I was like you at school. And look at me now."

"It's all right for you," Jen said.

"Why?"

"You're – pretty. You look nice. People probably like you just because of that."

"You think so? But I was exactly like you at school. I'd go days on end without speaking to anyone. I wouldn't look at anybody, because if I did, they'd start on me. I was wound up and on edge all the time. All the time."

Jen stared. "Yeah. That's what it's like."

"I got out," the woman said. "Not by running away, though. No, I left school as soon as I could. My parents wanted me to stay on, my teachers wanted me to stay on – but they were doing nothing to help. So I left. Got a job in a supermarket, filling fridges with butter and shelves with biscuits."

Jen was still staring. "I thought of being a vet," she said. You needed a lot of qualifications for that.

"Funny. So did I, at one time. But I got out, and started work, and you know what I found?"

"What?"

"That the people I worked with in the supermarket weren't anything like the nasty, spiteful, bubble-headed children I'd been penned up with at school. They were okay. They were easy-going. They were working for their living, and they had too many things to think about to care whether somebody else had the "right" mobile or the right pair of trainers. Everybody just rubbed along, were pretty friendly to everybody else, and did their job. I tell you, after being at school, working in that supermarket was like paradise."

"Honest?" Jen said.

"Honest. I'd thought, just like you, that it would be much the same as being at school, except I'd be paid, but it wasn't at all. I got on with people, and we had a laugh in the staff-room – I was very happy. Then I got sent on a management course. I wasn't too pleased about that, because I thought it'd be like going back to school, but

I thought I'd be brave and give it a go. I was so much happier, you see, it gave me a lot more confidence."

"And it was awful," Jen said, because she was sure it must have been.

"No! That's where you're wrong. The people were fine. They just wanted to get along with people, learn what they'd come to learn and pass the course. I found out something else too. I found that because I'd spent so much time on my own, I was used to it. I was more self-reliant than a lot of people. I didn't panic if I didn't have a bestest friend to go to class with – I just got on with everybody. And I did really well. I got promotion – that was just the start, but you don't want to hear about me climbing the ladder. Boring stuff. What I'm trying to tell you is, not all people are the same. I never tried moving to another school, but it might be that, if you did, you'd find a completely different bunch of people, a completely different atmosphere, and make a lot of friends."

"I don't know about that," Jen said. It seemed about as likely to her as making friends with Donna, Kayleigh and Lesley.

"I'll tell you what it is," the woman said. "You've got no confidence. That makes all the difference."

Jen half turned away. She'd heard all about "having

confidence in yourself" before, and she thought it was claptrap. How could you have confidence when you were short and boring, and called "stupid freak" because you didn't have the right clothes and didn't like the right pop groups?

"I used to look at grown-up people, who always seemed to know what to do and how to behave," said the woman, "and I used to think it was *because* they were grown-up. But I found out that you get confidence by trying to do something that you think you can't do, and finding that you can make some kind of a go of it anyway. Sometimes it takes a bit of practice. Now and again you make a real mess of things, but you find out that you live through it. After a while you find yourself thinking, "I can handle this" – because you've done something like it before. You get braver. What I'm trying to tell you, sweetheart, is that life gets better. I was a lot happier at twenty than I was at ten. And I'm happier at thirty than I was at twenty."

Jen turned and faced her. "Are you married?"

"No, but I live with a lovely man." The woman laughed. "I can't believe he was ever a little boy, because the boys I knew were so horrible and cruel, and he's so kind. I love him to bits."

"Have you got children?" Jen asked.

"Not yet. But I mean to have. Very soon." She looked at her watch. "Time's getting on. Do you want that lift?"

Jen jumped up. "No. Thanks, but – no, I'd better not."

The woman laughed. "Your mother's told you not to accept lifts from strangers, hasn't she? Quite right, too. You never should. But tell you what – let me walk home with you. Just in case Donna and co are lying in wait again."

"Okay," Jen said, and the woman rose from the bench. Together, they walked towards the park gates. "What's your name?" Jen asked, a little nervously, in case she was being rude.

"Jennifer," said the woman.

Jen looked up at her in surprise. "Same as mine!"

"Small world," said the woman.

As they turned out of the park gates, Jen said, "I live – "

"At number sixty-five, Hallcroft Road, Brackley. I know. I know the short cut there too."

Jen wondered how the woman knew. "Do I ... know you?"

"Not yet," the woman said, as they turned into the narrow lane. "You know, you feel hopeless because you think there's no way out, that things will never change, that you can only go on the way you are. But you're not a tram, love. You don't always have to run on the one set of tracks. If you don't like the track you're on, jump to another track. There's always a way to shake things up and change them. Always."

"Like, how?" Jen said.

"Like, scream and shout until somebody takes notice. Refuse to go to school."

"I can't!"

"Why not? What can anybody do?"

Jen cringed, thinking of the yelling and shouting, the weeks of sulks and bad temper from her mother.

"What are they going to do? Shout? Let them shout themselves hoarse. Hit you? You're getting hit at school, aren't you? Stop your pocket money? Do you care? Just tell them that, until they take you seriously and sort out this bullying, you're not going to school. Worth a try?"

"I can't," Jen said. But in the back of her mind, she was already planning how she would do it. She didn't think she would dare, but if –

"Never get trapped into thinking there's no other way and nothing you can do," the woman said, as they turned the corner into Hallcroft Road. "Do something. Anything. Throw things. Scream. Shout. If people won't help you, make them!"

They stopped outside Jen's house. Feeling stunned, her mind full of the scene that would take place next morning, when she refused to get up for school, Jen opened the gate. She thought what a relief it would be not to go to school, and not to meet Donna and Kayleigh and Lesley.

The woman called, "Remember; it's the squeaky wheel that gets the oil."

Jen remembered her manners. "Oh! Er – thank you. Thank you for everything, Miss – er – Jennifer."

The woman smiled. "My name," she said, "is Jennifer Appleby." She walked away briskly and turned the corner, leaving Jen standing at her front door.